What Makes Popcorn Pop?

Illustrations by
Ernest Albanese, Tanya Rebelo, John Rice,
Tom Powers, and Mimi Powers
Cover illustration by Tom Powers

Text copyright © 1991 by Highlights for Children
Illustrations copyright © 1991 by Boyds Mills Press
All rights reserved
Published by Bell Books
Boyds Mills Press, Inc.
A Highlights Company
815 Church Street
Honesdale, Pennsylvania 18431
Printed in China

Publisher Cataloging-in-Publication Data
Myers, Jack.
  What makes popcorn pop? : and other questions about the world around us /
answered by Highlights science editor Jack Myers.
[64]p. : col. ill. ; cm.
Includes index.
Summary : Dr. Jack Myers answers questions posed by children.
Many questions taken from columns in *Highlights for Children*.
ISBN 1-878093-33-9 HC ; ISBN 1-56397-402-9 PB
1. Science—Juvenile literature. [1. Science.] I. Series. II. Title.
500—dc20   1991
Library of Congress Catalog Card Number 90-85912

20 19 18 17 16 15 14 13

What Makes Popcorn Pop?

And Other Questions About The World Around Us

Answered by

Highlights Science Editor
Jack Myers, Ph.D.

BOYDS MILLS PRESS

Welcome Aboard!

You have joined our club. We are the curious, wondering about all the interesting things that happen in our world. When we don't know, we ask. Here in the records of our club you will find answers to some of the questions you have wondered about.

For the past thirty years readers of Highlights for Children have been asking me questions. And I have been helping them find answers. There have been questions I could not answer and questions that I think no one could answer. Science has always been like that, and it is like that today even in the world's greatest laboratories. It is our ignorance—what we don't know—that drives us to learn more. That's what science is all about.

I have been fortunate in having as friends many scientists who have helped me find answers. To all of them we are grateful, for they have broadened our understanding.

Jack Myers, Ph.D.

What makes popcorn pop?

Kimberly Gail Anderson
Alma, Arkansas

Popcorn is a special kind of corn. One thing that makes it special is that each grain has a thin, but very tight coat. When you heat it up, the little bit of water inside turns to steam. Because the steam can't get out through the coat, the whole grain of corn explodes.

Good popping popcorn must have just the right moisture content so there will be just the right amount of steam in the grains and all of them will pop.

Happy popping. I like it, too.

5

Since salt is not hot, how does it melt ice and snow?

Michael Gray
Guelph, Ontario

The freezing point of water, the temperature just cold enough to make it freeze into ice, is 0 degrees Celsius. Dissolving salt in water makes the water harder to freeze. To get salt water to freeze you have to make it colder than 0 degrees. So you can say that salt lowers the freezing point of water.

If you add salt to ice, some of the salt will melt. You can suppose that the salt pulls some water away from its crystal form in ice. When that happens the ice-salt mixture will get colder than 0 degrees.

Here is a recipe for making a very cold freezing mixture: Mix 33 ounces of salt with 100 ounces of snow or finely crushed ice. That is supposed to give a temperature of minus 21 degrees C.

When you put dry ice and warm water together, why does smoke pour out of the container? And why does dry ice put out fire?

Abby Hosford
Gainesville, Georgia

Dry ice is interesting stuff. It is frozen carbon dioxide. Its temperature is about minus 79 degrees Celsius. When it is warmed, instead of turning into a liquid, it turns right into a gas. A single teaspoon of dry ice will make several quarts of pure carbon dioxide gas.

Now we can think about the answers to your questions. When you drop a piece of dry ice into warm water, it rapidly turns into gas and bubbles out. As it does, it carries some water vapor out into the air. Then some of the water vapor condenses into droplets and appears as steam.

Carbon dioxide is good for putting out fires if it surrounds the fire and keeps oxygen away. So liquid carbon dioxide is held under pressure in some fire extinguishers and kept just for use on a fire. Since carbon dioxide is a heavy gas—heavier than air—it works best on a fire in a low place.

Dry ice is fun, but also dangerous. You should never try to pick it up with your fingers. It will cause frostbite just as bad as a burn.

If heat makes things expand and cold makes them contract, why does water expand when you freeze it?

Jenny Tudesko
Sacramento, California

Water is very common. But in some ways it is also very strange and different than anything else we know.

Water is strangest when it is a liquid, as we usually see it. Because its molecules are so sticky to each other, they find ways to snuggle in tightly to each other and still move around.

When water freezes, its molecules lock themselves into a special pattern of six-sided figures. In that pattern the molecules take up more room than they did in the liquid. So water expands as it freezes from liquid water into crystals of ice.

Why does ice last longer on a hot day if you wrap it in something?

Nathan Bennett
Tulsa, Oklahoma

Let's think about the problem this way. Ice melts because heat flows to it from something else. The heat makes the ice melt. And something else that gave up the heat gets colder.

Some materials carry heat very readily and we say that they are good conductors. Most metals, especially copper, are good conductors. Other materials do not carry heat very well and we call them insulators. To keep ice from melting we want to surround it with an insulator.

Just wrapping newspapers around a piece of ice slows the melting. The newspaper is a pretty good insulator, at least until it gets soppy wet.

Why do the sun and moon seem to follow me when I'm riding in a car?

Joshua Woehrer
Milwaukee, Wisconsin

I think everyone has had that feeling. When you are traveling in a car, buildings, fences, and signs go by you in a hurry but the sun or moon just seem to hang up there as if they were following you. This happens because the sun and the moon are so very far away—thousands of times farther than anything you can see on earth.

The farther away something is the more slowly it seems to move. Here's a simple way to see that. Watch a bird swoosh by as it flies across your yard. Then watch a jet plane high in the sky. The plane may be flying at almost four hundred miles an hour, but it seems to move very slowly because it is several miles away. The bird is flying only about a tenth as fast as a jet plane but it goes by in a hurry because it is so much closer.

Our eyes give us pictures of the world around us. But our eyes don't tell us enough about how far away things are. That part we have to get used to.

What makes stars shine and sometimes blink?

Karla Lindula
Auburn, Washington

We think that stars shine because each of them is a big hot glowing ball of gas like our sun. So just think of stars as suns—but very much farther away.

That twinkle does not come from the star itself. Light from the star comes to our eyes through a thick layer of air around our earth. Light goes right through that air layer, but it gets twisted back and forth just a little as it goes through winds and hot and cold layers up there. So the little beam of light from a star gets jumbled enough to make the star seem to twinkle.

That twinkling is a big problem for astronomers. You can see why they put their telescopes on high mountains so they do not have to look through such a thick layer of air.

If we have two eyes, how come we don't see double?

Abby Myers
Wilkes-Barre, Pennsylvania

The direction of each of your eyes is controlled by three pairs of muscles connected to the outside of the eyeball. These are the most precisely controlled muscles of your body. They are controlled by nerve messages from the brain to keep your eyes pointed together.

Seeing begins with nerve messages sent by light-sensitive cells in the retina at the back of each eye and ending up in your brain. That all works so that your brain "sees" a picture of the little image that falls on the retina. And the eyes are pointed together so carefully that the same picture is formed by messages from your two eyes. That's how you can use two eyes to see "single" and not "double."

9

How does a plant grow by just planting it in the mud?

Benjamin Orgeron
Harvey, Louisiana

I never thought of plants as being unusual, but when you say it that way maybe they are.

I suppose you are thinking about planting a seed. That's really a baby or embryo plant with some stored food material around it, carefully protected by a tough coat. It will stay that way, sometimes for years as long as it is kept dry.

The seed changes when it gets warm and moist. Then it starts to grow and bursts out of the tough coat. It makes a root that grows downward and a stem that grows upward.

All this depends on the food material stored in the seed, which lasts until the little plant has made some green leaves. Then it can use sunlight to make its own food.

So, for a plant, warm mud is really a good place to begin life.

When I asked my dad why an apple turns brown when you take a bite out of it or why a banana turns brown when you peel it, he said it had something to do with oxygen and the fruit. Could you explain?

Jane Bradshaw
Rockport, Texas

Your dad is correct. The darkening actually needs three different things: oxygen, tyrosine, and an enzyme called tyrosinase. You know about oxygen. Tyrosine is an amino acid, one of the things used to build protein. Some of it is present in almost all living tissues.

Tyrosinase is an enzyme. That means it has the power to speed up some special chemical reaction. By themselves, oxygen and tyrosine react so slowly that you would get tired watching them to see anything happen. But if just a few molecules of tyrosinase are around, there is a rapid chemical reaction. Oxygen combines with tyrosine molecules and ties them together to make a dark stuff called melanin. That's why a cut apple darkens. And the same thing happens to a cut banana or potato.

You might be interested to know that melanin is a very common dark pigment formed also in the skin or hairs or feathers of animals.

Some friends who are good cooks tell me that there is an easy way to keep apples from darkening when you cut them up for a salad. Sprinkle on a little lemon juice. That contains ascorbic acid (also called vitamin C), which prevents the oxidation of tyrosine. Why don't you try this and see if the lemon juice will slow down the darkening of a cut apple?

Why do pine trees keep their leaves in winter?

Ivan Middleton
Adrian, Michigan

You probably have noticed that the trees which keep their leaves through the winter— like the pines, spruces, and firs—have special leaves that are like tough little needles. These have a lot less water than the thin, flat leaves that fall from other trees in autumn.

Those needlelike leaves of the pine tree also have a special ability to stand below-freezing temperatures without damage. Most organisms that can do that have some special "antifreeze" chemicals.

Scientists are learning more about these. The big danger of freezing is the formation of ice crystals which push right through cell membranes and kill the tissue. Some of the "antifreeze" chemicals work to prevent the formation of ice crystals. I think that's a neat trick.

11

I pushed my finger into a soap bubble, but it didn't pop. Why not?

Patricia West
Birmingham, Alabama

Soap bubbles are surprising in the way they behave. And there are many interesting things you can do with them.

Soap bubbles pop when the film of soap and water around them gets stretched too thin or if the water in the film evaporates. If you were in a bathtub your fingers probably were wet and soapy. Touching a soap bubble with a dry object is more likely to break it.

Why do you need two holes to pour juice out of a can?

Philomena Zito
Pomona, New Jersey

This happens because the pressure of air around us pushes inward against the hole. This actually is much greater than the pressure of the juice trying to get out. You would need a juice can about thirty-two feet tall to give the juice at the hole enough pressure to force itself out against the air pressure.

When you make a second hole you give air a way to get in and bubble up inside the can. Then air pressure is working about equally both inside and outside the can. And the pressure of the juice makes it run out of the lowest hole.

Maybe another way to say all this is that you need two holes, one to let the juice out and one to let air in. Of course, just one big hole also will work because it can let air bubble in and juice come out, too.

I was drinking a can of soda through a straw. I put my index finger on top of the straw and lifted it up. The soda would not pour out of the straw until I lifted my finger. Why?

Roslyn Davis
East Hartford, Connecticut

The soda is held up and can't leave unless air can get in to take its place. Your finger on top of the straw seals it off against air pressure from that direction. But air pressure pushing upward is just as great as the weight of the water pushing downward. When you take your finger away, air pressure pushes equally on the top and bottom of the straw. Then the soda's weight makes it run out.

Chemists use that same trick to measure and transfer solutions. They use glass tubes called pipettes.

How come when you drop something into a bottle of soda, bubbles come up and make the soda spill all over the place?

Chris Coleman
Montgomery, Alabama

Soda water is made by dissolving carbon dioxide gas in water or in a flavored solution. This is done under pressure and then the bottle is capped.

When you take off the cap and release the pressure, carbon dioxide wants to come out of the solution and make bubbles. Unless the bottle is warmed or shaken, this usually will happen slowly. The soda water will keep its soda (carbon dioxide) long enough to taste good while you drink it.

Most things that you might drop into the bottle, especially if they have rough surfaces or sharp edges, help the carbon dioxide come out of the solution and form bubbles faster.

13

What causes a shock, and how come it makes blue sparks?

Blair Priest
Towson, Maryland

I think you are talking about static electricity which you might generate by walking over a thick carpet. Your shoes rubbing against carpet fibers give you an electric charge by picking up extra electrons from the carpet. Then when you touch something like a doorknob the extra electrons leave in a hurry and you feel a little shock.

If all this happens in a darkened room, then you also may see a little spark that goes with the shock. And I think you are right: the spark looks blue. Before your fingers actually touch the doorknob some of your charged-up electricity jumps across through the air. That makes the spark.

Air does not carry electricity very well. It is a good insulator—until you get a great enough voltage over a short distance. Then some of the molecules of air become ionized, meaning that they become electrically charged.

Every kind of atom has its own characteristic color. You have seen the red color of neon signs made by ionized atoms of neon gas inside. Air is mostly nitrogen, and I think the blue color of the spark comes from ionized nitrogen atoms.

When electricity makes things hot, does the electricity get hot?

Jenny Stoops
Brownsburg, Indiana

Electricity is a form of energy, not an object that takes up space. When electricity passes through anything, even a copper wire, some of it is lost and appears in another form of energy which we call heat. You can use electricity to heat an electric iron. Some of the electricity is used up to make heat so that the iron gets hot.

You can say the same thing about light. Think of a sidewalk on a sunny day. Sunlight falling upon it is absorbed and changed into heat. So the sidewalk gets warmer.

You may think this is all a little bit tricky. We can say that electricity can be changed into heat. But we do not say that electricity gets hot.

How are tapes made for a tape recorder?

Michael Zions
Far Rockaway, New York

We can transfer the sounds of your voice into changes in an electric current, and then transfer the changes of electric current back into sound. That's what a telephone does. That's how a tape recorder works, too.

What a tape must do is to "remember" the changes in electric current so we can play them back and listen to them later.

The tape remembers with its thousands of tiny magnetic particles. The recording head is an electromagnet. As the tape passes over the head, a changing electric current arranges the magnetic particles in a special pattern. Then, when you pull the tape back across the head, you set up the same special pattern of electric current which can be turned back into sound.

Of course, we can also record much more complicated things—like a whole movie. But the idea is always the same.

Why can't you see the wind?

Shannon Clonch
Reynoldsburg, Ohio

I wondered why you would ask that question. Maybe it is because you can *feel* the wind. So why can't you see it?

The answer is so simple that it isn't much fun. You can't see the air around you. And wind is only moving air. So you can't see the wind, either.

Maybe you would like to turn the question around. If we can't see the air, how do we know it's there? Because we can feel it when it moves as wind. If there were no air, planes and birds couldn't fly— and you couldn't breathe.

Where does the wind come from?

Ben Bowen
Orlando, Florida

You know that the earth is kept warm by sunlight. But the earth is not warmed evenly over all of its surface. At any one time about half is in sunlight during the day and the other half is in the shade which we call night. And since the earth is an almost-round ball, there will always be some part (near the equator) on which sunlight hits head on and other parts (near the poles) where sunlight hits at an angle.

Above any warm spot on the earth's surface, the air is heated. Warm air expands to become lighter, and it rises. So there are always some places where air is expanding and rising and some places where air is cooling and moving downward.

This uneven heating and cooling is enough to start air in motion to make wind. Then a lot of other things happen. Air moving over the ocean picks up lots of water vapor. Then if that air gets cooled, it forms clouds. So the air above us is always churning around to give us all the changes that the weatherman talks about.

16

Why does dust seem to move along a beam of sunlight in the same direction as the light?

Tiffany Sharp
Kansas City, Missouri

I have watched dust particles in a beam of sunlight in the way you suggest. Sometimes it does seem as if dust particles are moving in the direction of the light beam. However, I think that is likely to be just an accident, or maybe our eyes fool us.

Light does exert a very small pressure, but this is so small that there is no simple way to show it. Particles in the air are moved about mainly by small air currents. The push of light on a dust particle is much smaller than the push of even very small air movements.

What is house dust?

Diana Hedgpeth
Torrance, California

House dust has lots of things in it and just what it contains probably differs in different houses. Because it has such fine particles, you would need a microscope to see what is there. As in most dust, it is likely to have tiny particles of soil or sand, pollen dust from flowers, and spores produced by micro-organisms such as molds. It is also likely to have little fibers of lint from rugs and clothing and hair. Some people get asthma or allergies like hay fever from house dust.

How come when I am out in the sun my skin gets darker but my shirt fades?

Kelly Holt
Willsboro, New York

You've made an interesting observation. There are many photochemical reactions—chemical reactions brought about by light. Many colored materials absorb light and help bring about photochemical reactions which change them and destroy their color. That happens to many dyes used to color our clothes.

Sunlight, especially the ultraviolet part of it, is bad for living cells because it causes many destructive photochemical reactions. One of these gives you sunburn. Your skin tries to help protect you by making a dark pigment called melanin. Melanin acts as a screen in absorbing light close to the surface of your skin. Dark skin already has a lot of melanin. And some people form melanin and get tanned more easily than others. However, overexposure to sunlight is not good for anyone.

Are black and white colors?

Jaime Foster
Rock Island, Illinois

I think you might get either a yes or a no answer on this, depending on what someone is thinking about when answering the question.

If you are a printer with different color inks, black ink would be one of them. And of the different papers you might choose, one would be white.

But I would say no, they are not colors. Something white, like snow or white paper, is white because it reflects light of all colors equally. And something black, like coal, is black because it absorbs light of all colors equally. Something that is colored, like a rose, will be red if it reflects red light and absorbs light of other colors.

You can see why I think the answer is no. But I would not like to argue about this question with a printer.

Why does black absorb heat better than other colors?

Sumana Reddy
Norcross, Georgia

Black is black because it absorbs all colors of light. And absorbed light is turned into heat. So if you want something to warm up in sunlight, paint it black.

Now I can ask you. What color would you paint an object which you want to stay as cool as possible in sunlight?

19

Sometimes in the afternoon I see the moon. Why is this?

Alicia Mosialis
Woodbury, Minnesota

The moon is going around the earth in a big circle all the time. We can see it only when it is up above our side of the earth. And we see it because of the light that falls on it from the sun.

When the moon is up above us at night it seems to glow brightly because of the dark sky behind it. When it is up above us during the day it glows just as brightly. But then the sky behind it is so bright that we usually do not even notice it. You must have been looking carefully to see it in the afternoon.

What causes tides?

Kenneth Weaver
Grand Prairie, Texas

I can't tell you all about tides, but I can tell you the basic idea. The tides are caused by the effect of the force of gravity of the moon. The actual pull of the moon's gravity isn't very great. You can't feel the moon when it goes overhead, but it does have a small effect in a special way.

Since the earth is a solid body, the pull of the moon's gravity acts upon the center of the earth. The ocean is at the earth's surface, so it is four thousand miles closer to the moon than the core of the earth. So when the moon is overhead, it pulls on the water more than on the earth. This makes the water bunch up a little under the moon. That's what is called a high tide.

If you look up "tides" in an encyclopedia, you can learn a lot more about them.

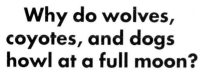

Why do wolves, coyotes, and dogs howl at a full moon?

Justyna Piasecka
Washington, D.C.

I have never seen a very satisfying explanation of that question. In fact, I'm not sure just why they howl at all. Of course, wolves in the wild hunt in packs. So howling might be a way of telling each other where they are.

I can't think of a good reason why a full moon would make any difference. I wonder if that part is really true. Maybe it's just an idea that people talk about but don't bother to see if it is true.

If you find a better answer to your question, please let me know.

When you hit or touch something, why does it make a sound?

Sara Clark
Owaneco, Illinois

If you hit your desktop with a pencil you set up some vibrations, some in the desktop and some in the pencil. These vibrations set up vibrations in air that are carried in the air to your ears. Your ear can hear vibrations like that. We call them sound.

How does that sound to you?

How come if you go into the bathroom to sing it sounds better than when you are in the bedroom or anywhere else?

Glonar Fonseca
Lemoore, California

I congratulate you on having a good singing voice. I used to try singing in the bathroom and it sounded great to me. But my family never thought it was much of an improvement.

I think bathroom singing is special and may make your voice sound better. Bathrooms, especially around tubs and shower stalls, have bare walls that make nice crisp echoes and reverberations. That gives your voice extra quality.

One day I was looking at stained glass and I wondered, "How do they stain it?"

Courtney Bennett
Newtown, Pennsylvania

Glass is made by heating compounds of silicon until they melt or fuse. When the hot liquid cools down, it forms glass. Sand (mostly silicon dioxide) can be used by itself, but it needs a very high temperature to be melted. With the addition of some other chemicals, glass can be made at a lower temperature. Sodium carbonate is added to make most window glass, lead oxide to make most crystal, and sodium borate to make Pyrex.

People have been making glass for over a thousand years. At some time along the way they learned that other kinds of minerals melted in with glass would give it special colors. Ruby glass contains copper, blue glass contains cobalt, and green glass usually contains iron. That's what we call stained glass.

Some of the famous stained-glass windows of cathedrals in Europe were made about six hundred years ago. No one knew much about chemistry then, but they found out, just by testing, what minerals to add to get different colors.

I think it is interesting that people learned to make glass and even some of the world's most beautiful stained glass before they knew much of anything about its chemistry.

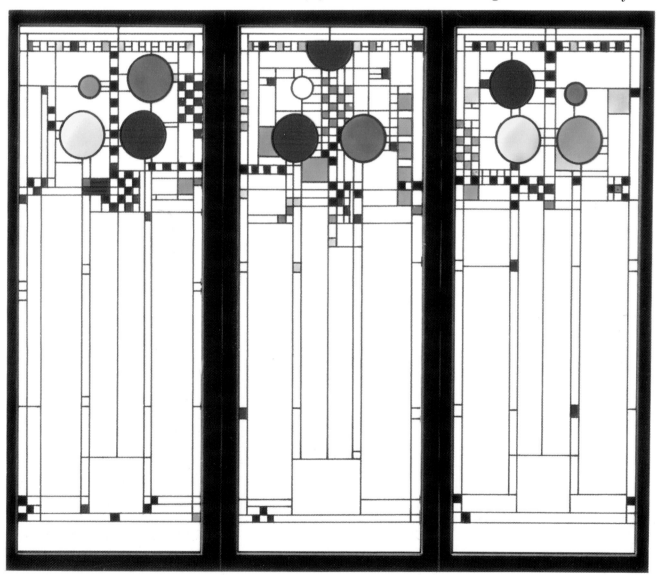

Why does ice stick to cotton?

Tienda Greene
Pikesville, Maryland

It's easy to make ice stick to cotton, but something special must happen. There must be a little water to wet the cotton. This may come from the surface of an ice cube where it is melted just a little by warmer air. And the ice cube, maybe right out of the freezer, must be at a temperature below freezing.

If both those things happen, then the ice cube freezes the water that wets the cotton. So the cotton sticks because it is frozen right to the ice cube.

Why do ice cubes float?

Michael Sciortino
Homer, New York

The fact that ice cubes float on water tells us something important about water. When water freezes and changes into a solid, its molecules arrange themselves so that they occupy more space.

Another way to think about it is that a quart of ice weighs less than a quart of water. The ice is lighter, so it floats.

Most liquid substances contract and occupy less space when they change to their solid forms. For example, a piece of solid lead sinks if dropped into a pot of hot melted lead.

How come you can't see water evaporating?

Sharon Vig
London, Ontario

When water evaporates, water molecules are leaving the surface of the liquid water and going out into the air as a gas which we call water vapor. Water vapor is a colorless gas, so you can't see it in the air. And each molecule is so very tiny that it would take about a million billion billion to fill a tablespoon. So you can't see any effect on the water surface as they leave one by one.

I never thought about it like this before, but I guess you could say that evaporation of water is pretty sneaky.

Why does water ripple when you throw a rock into it?

Danny Anisfeld
Westlake Village, California

I guess we all have chucked rocks into a lake or pond just to watch the ripple or wave they make. On a quiet surface there is a neat circle of a wave that travels outward, getting to be a bigger and bigger circle. You want to know how it gets started.

I think the best way to answer that is to drop a small rock in a pool of water that you can get up close to and see what happens.

I used a big kitchen sink. I wish it had been bigger. I let the surface get quiet and then dropped in a small stone. When you do this, you will need to watch carefully because everything happens quickly.

Here is what I think happens. As the stone goes through the surface it pushes water out of the way and makes a ring of water that bulges above the surface. Then, as the stone passes, water from the bulge rushes in to where the stone had been. I was surprised to see a little fountain of water come back up where the stone had been. All that was followed quickly by the ring of a little wave. I think it was the little fountain that started the wave but I could not be sure.

Why don't you try this? Maybe your eyes will be better than mine at seeing what really happens.

I know that rubber balls bounce because, as the ball hits the ground, the rubber dents and springs back, pushing the ball into the air. But why do hard things like marbles bounce?

David Johnson
Williamson, West Virginia

The bounciness of something depends on what we call its elasticity. Elastic materials are those that can be squeezed or bent or dented or stretched and then return to the size or shape they had before. Some materials, like butter, seem to have no elasticity at all.

Most of us think of rubber as being elastic. We can stretch a rubber band or bounce a rubber ball. Of course, air is elastic, too. If we squeeze or compress air it tries to expand again. So air pumped into a rubber cover makes a good bouncy basketball.

Now what about hard things like glass and steel? They are elastic, too. Think about the steel wire used to make the "strings" of a piano. When tapped, they vibrate to make a musical sound. A piano is tuned by stretching each string so that it vibrates at the right pitch. Piano wire is elastic. It is also very hard. One of the common ways to use the elasticity of steel is in springs made by coiling up wire.

Steel ball bearings are very bouncy when they hit together. Each ball is dented, ever so little, but bounces back to its round shape. Glass marbles are hard and elastic in the same way. Hard glass and steel are much more elastic than softer materials like wood or aluminum.

Why are some solid materials hard and elastic and others soft and more buttery? This seems to depend on how tightly the molecules of the substances hold to each other. Suppose the molecules of a substance stick together very tightly. Then it is difficult to push them out of their positions, and the substance is hard. If the molecules do get pushed out of position, they tend to snap back, so the substance is also elastic.

If this explanation is right, then what should we think about rubber? It is soft, but also elastic. We think this is because of the special shape of its molecules. Each rubber molecule is long and kinky and maybe looped around its neighbor. So rubber is elastic because each of its molecules is stretchy. Rubber is a special and unusual substance, soft and easy to stretch but also elastic.

How come people use air to blow out small fires, but also use it to make large fires bigger?

Elise Morrison
Hobbs, New Mexico

I have noticed that, too. And at first it does seem to be a surprise. Air does two opposite things to a fire. It provides oxygen that is needed for anything to burn. If you keep air from getting to a fire, you can put it out.

Air also can cool down a fire. The flame and heat of a fire come from burning gases. A blast of air hard enough to keep the flame away from the fuel will put out a fire.

I guess this is another case of "a little is great, but too much is bad."

When my dad strikes a match, a flame appears. Why?

Lillie Wade
Alexandria, Virginia

A match is a special kind of invention for making fire. The idea is the same as the old trick of twirling a stick round and round while pressing its end into a rounded-out spot in another piece of wood. The friction makes the end of the stick get hot. If some easy-to-burn stuff like wood shavings is right there, it could get hot enough to begin burning.

The head of a match usually has a chemical, like potassium chlorate, and some charcoal or sulfur. The striking surface may have some red phosphorus and fine sand. The idea is to get heat by friction and have something there that is very easy to burn. That's a lot easier than the stick trick.

One cold winter night I was sitting by the radiator when I wondered what kept hot air running through it.

Tracy Thomas
Horseheads, New York

There are two kinds of radiators commonly used in houses. One kind has an open grill in the floor or wall with big pipes that bring up hot air from a furnace that is usually in the basement. The hot air may be pushed up by a fan inside. Or sometimes just one or two extra-large pipes from the furnace carry air upward. Warm air is lighter (or less dense) so it tends to rise all by itself.

There is also another kind of radiator that sits in a room and is connected to the furnace by water pipes. Hot water comes up from a furnace below and slowly circulates upward through the radiator and back again. This may have a pump, but usually the water moves because hot water is lighter and tends to rise to the radiator. Then it gets cooler in the radiator and sinks back in another pipe toward the furnace.

So we can use the trick that warmer air or water is lighter to carry heat from a furnace to all the rooms of a house.

If heat rises, why is it cold on top of mountains?

Maggie Ehrgott
Marshall, Washington

You are right that warm air rises. The main place air is heated is at the earth's surface, where it is warmed by sunlight. So there are always updrafts of rising hot air above us.

As we go up in the atmosphere, air pressure continually becomes less. That means the rising air is expanding. And a characteristic of any gas is that it is cooled by expansion. So the draft of warm air that starts rising from the earth's surface continually cools itself as it rises. The temperature goes down three or four degrees Fahrenheit for every thousand feet higher we go.

28

How does a fan cool a room? I thought moving particles made heat.

Jim Vere
Flemington, New Jersey

You are right that stirring or mixing up any fluid, whether water or air, always warms it a little. A small desk fan makes about as much heat as a 100-watt light bulb. However, by moving the air other things happen, too.

Sometimes we use fans to pull in outside air that may be cooler than the air inside. But even in a closed room, moving air will help keep us cool. Moving air helps to evaporate sweat from your skin more rapidly. That's an important way our body has to try to keep cool on a hot day.

So the idea is that, even though a fan makes a little heat, it also does other things that help to make you feel cool.

On really hot days, most of the kids in my class fan ourselves with notebooks. Our teacher says fanning yourself just makes you hotter. Why?

Deborah Rosen
Albany, New York

You may often see people fanning themselves on a hot day when they must sit somewhere that has no air movement. They certainly must think that fanning makes them feel cooler. However, I can see how the answer to your question could go either way.

Moving air cools your skin by evaporating a little sweat. That may happen even when you can't see any sweat at all. In fact, the main use of sweat by your body is to try to keep it cool. And that works better in moving air than in quiet air.

But there is also another part of the problem. It takes energy to move air. Fanning yourself means that some of the muscles in your hand and arm are working. Whenever your muscles work, they also make extra heat. That tends to make you warmer.

You can see that if fanning makes more muscle heat than you lose by faster evaporation of sweat, then fanning will actually make you warmer.

29

What would happen to a glass of water if you dumped it in space?

Christa Giordano
Philadelphia, Pennsylvania

I think it would just seem to explode and disappear. Space has a condition that you can call a "high vacuum"—almost no air at all. All those water molecules suddenly would have no more neighbors to bump into, so they would just fly apart in space.

How are shooting stars made?

*Bobbie Petersen
Tracy, California*

Most of the stuff in our solar system is in big bodies: the sun and planets and moons. There are also some rather small pieces of stuff as small as grains of sand or as large as big boulders. They are called meteoroids. I guess you can think of them as the trash of our solar system.

We know about meteoroids because some of them are on paths that make them run into our earth. Then the friction of the earth's atmosphere makes them white hot. We see them for a second or so until they vaporize, or burn up. That is the pretty sight you call a meteor or a shooting star.

Once in a while a big meteoroid does not all burn up and a piece of it falls all the way to the ground. The piece that is left is called a meteorite.

30

Why are there constellations?

Michelle Trautman
Scotts Valley, California

I'm not sure just how to answer your question. You did not ask why there are stars. Really, you want to know why people invented certain patterns out of the stars that we know as constellations.

It's my guess that people have always been fascinated by the heavens. Back when life was simpler, people generally lived by the sun, working during daylight hours. Many people were in close touch with nature. Surely a great many spent evenings talking with their friends and amusing themselves. One of the ways they passed their time at night, no doubt, was looking at the stars. I'll bet they found it fun to make up constellations.

I like to imagine a shepherd out guarding his flock on a lonely hill passing the time by thinking about certain patterns he saw. These patterns came to be shared by a number of people through the years and are now fairly common. But if you think about it, you could really make up your own.

31

How does a magnet attract metal?

Andrea Caron
Greenfield Park, Quebec

Actually, magnetism is a special property found in only a few metals, especially in iron and somewhat in cobalt and nickel.

Magnetism is a big subject, but maybe I can give you some ideas about it.

There is an important relationship between electricity and magnetism. Electricity is the movement of electrons. Any moving electron behaves as if it has a magnetic field—a cloud of magnetism—around it.

In all atoms there is a central nucleus with outer electrons spinning around in an orderly way. Different kinds of elements have atoms with different numbers and arrangements of those outer electrons. Do those spinning electrons create magnetic fields? We believe that they do. However, in most kinds of atoms the spins of the many electrons do not work together. You could say that they cancel each other so that the whole atom is not magnetic.

In an atom of iron it just happens that some of its electrons spin together just right. Their effects add together and the whole atom or a cluster of atoms behaves as a small magnet. A whole iron or steel bar behaves as a magnet if we can get all its little clusters of atoms lined up just right and working together.

You can think of any magnet as having a magnetic field or "cloud of magnetism" around it. If a piece of iron is close by, it is drawn toward the magnet. Maybe we can think that the atoms of that piece of iron are lined up, sort of soak up the cloud, and are pulled toward the magnet.

The ideas of magnetism make up a big and fascinating subject which I hope you will study. Someday, when you have learned a great deal more about it, you will think that the explanation I gave you here is way too simple.

Can you make gold from natural resources?

Heather Browning
Orland Park, Illinois

Very simply, the answer is no. Gold is one of the elements, and one of the important ideas of chemistry is that you can't change one element into another. There are some exceptions to this in the radioactive elements and in the special conditions that happen in the very high temperatures of stars. But gold is not one of the exceptions.

The modern idea about the elements was learned two hundred years ago. The science of chemistry grew out of an older practice called alchemy which had gone on for more than a thousand years. One of the main goals of alchemy was to make gold from other materials.

No one has been able to make gold out of anything else, even though people tried for over a thousand years. So I don't think you want to try it.

Why does metal feel cooler than wood when both are the same temperature?

John Fuery
Oakland, California

Some materials, like most metals, are good conductors and allow heat to flow very easily. Other things like wood and glass and Styrofoam are poor conductors.

When you touch something cold it feels cold because it takes some heat away from your hand. So you can see that a good conductor like aluminum takes heat away faster than a poor conductor like wood.

Why do we shiver?

Stephanie Allen
Gainesville, Virginia

Shivering is a special way the body has of trying to warm up when it gets cold. Whenever your muscles are working, they are also giving off heat. You already know this because when you are running or playing hard you get warm. Then your body sweats, and this helps cool you by evaporation of the sweat.

When your body gets cold you can help it warm up by running or some other kind of exercise. If you do not do that, your body has its own automatic or reflex way of making muscles work just under your skin. That is what we call shivering.

What causes you to breathe without thinking about it?

Jennifer Archer
Hickory, North Carolina

We are lucky that our bodies have a number of automatic controls to keep all our machinery working right. Many of these control our inside machinery and we never know about them. You can tell about some of them—like the control of the heart—by feeling your pulse.

Breathing is interesting because it can be controlled in two ways. You can decide when to breathe. You can breathe extra fast or you can even hold your breath for a short time. But when you are not thinking about it, your automatic control takes over. So you don't have to spend a lot of time worrying about when to take another breath.

The control point for your automatic control is in the base of your brain. It gets nerve messages from many places in your body. And it regulates the breathing muscles in your chest. It makes your breathing speed up during exercise and slow down when you are resting.

Our bodies are not all alike, but when we are at rest our most common breathing rate is fourteen times a minute.

34

Sometimes I have a funny feeling that someone is watching me, or I think I'm being followed. I turn out to be right almost every time. How can people "sense" that they are being watched?

Debra Burton
Delta, British Columbia

Your question got me a little curious. I guess I have felt sometimes that there was a person behind me, and I think I could agree that my experience is like yours— sometimes they are, some- times they are not. I think when a person is behind you, you probably get a number of messages. You may hear a slight movement. You might detect a special odor like a perfume. Even though none of these might lead you to believe the person was there, you later discover it is true.

Sometimes you think some- one is following you or behind you when actually no one is there. You may have misread some clues. Or it is possible that your mind is just playing little tricks on you. I'm not sure that any of this is really a scientific explanation. I hope it's of some help, though.

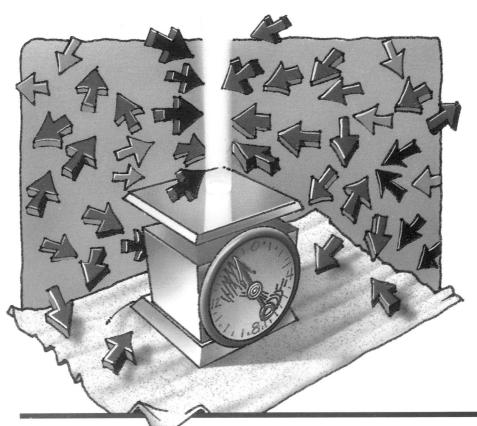

Since air is matter, does gravity hold the air down around us?

Jessica Bassett
Wellfleet, Massachusetts

The answer is yes. Our blanket of air actually is a weight pressing against the earth. We say that the air around us has a pressure of fifteen pounds per square inch. (A square inch is an area just about the size of a fifty-cent piece.) We could also say that all the air above each square inch of the earth's surface weighs fifteen pounds. That is a measure of the effect of gravity on air.

I would like to know how the earth floats in space and doesn't fall like a ball would fall.

Alicia Saylor
Hollsopple, Pennsylvania

If the earth were really alone it would actually just float in space. There would be no place to fall to.

But the earth is not alone. Fortunately it is locked into an orbit around the sun, held there by the force of gravity. You can think of the earth's motion this way. It is always trying to fall toward the sun. But because it is whirling around the sun in a circular path, it is also always trying to whirl out into space. Those two forces work against each other perfectly to keep the earth in its orbit.

When you are sitting on a bike with your feet off the ground and not pedaling, why does the bike tend to fall?

April Billet
Quartz Hill, California

Of course you always have to balance yourself when you are on a bike. That's easy when you are pedaling, but harder when you are stopped. When you are pedaling, the wheels are spinning. That makes your bike a gyroscope. A wheel spinning in an upright position tends to keep that position.

That same idea also works for other things. You have noticed that a spinning top falls over when it stops spinning.

So here's a question for a trivia game: how are bicycles and tops alike?

If we had no gravity, would a balloon fall to the ground?

Haley Shupe
Amanda, Ohio

You know that a balloon floats upward if it weighs less than the same volume of air. Weighing less means that the pull of the earth's gravity is less. If there were no such thing as gravity, there would be no force of gravity pulling on the balloon. So the balloon would not fall to the ground. That's one way to answer your question.

In our everyday lives we see the effect of gravity as a force pulling everything toward the center of the earth. However, you should remember that gravity is an important property of matter that works everywhere. Every body attracts every other body.

So we ought to consider that there is a lot more to your "what-if" question. If there were no force of gravity our world would be very different. There would be nothing to hold a blanket of air around the earth. In fact, there could be no earth if there were no force of gravity to hold it together.

The force of gravity is such an important part of nature that it is hard to imagine how things would be without it.

Why can't we see the minerals in the ocean until the water evaporates?

Kathy Steele
Guymon, Oklahoma

Seawater is a solution. That means that all the molecules present move around so happily together that there are no boundaries between different parts. That's another easy way of saying that inside the solution there are no places that can bend or reflect light. So the solution is perfectly clear.

If we take the water away by letting its molecules escape into the air, then the salts are left behind as crystals. Now there are boundaries at the surface of each crystal and it's easy to see the salts.

When a quart of seawater loses all its water by evaporation, it will leave about an ounce or about a tablespoon of salt. Most of that is sodium chloride, the same stuff that is in the saltshaker on your table.

How come when you put water on sand it moves a little bit, but then freezes?

Kathy Latirira
Barre, Vermont

That's an interesting observation. You noticed a special property of sand-water mixtures. It even has a fancy name: thixotropy. In a stirred or flowing sand-water mixture the sand particles act like independent little balls. Once the movement stops, the sand particles settle together in a "comfortable" position and stick to each other. They become so firm that they are sometimes called a gel, meaning something almost solid like gelatin.

Some kinds of sand do this more readily than others. Now you know what makes "quicksand" behave as it does.

I was at the Smithsonian space exhibit, and I am wondering how they freeze-dry space food.

Lee Anne Meck
Lititz, Pennsylvania

Freeze-drying is a special way of drying stuff. First you freeze it very rapidly at low temperature. The idea is to turn all the water quickly into very tiny ice crystals. Then you pump all the air away and keep the food in a vacuum. Then water molecules leave the ice crystals as water vapor without ever forming liquid water.

Ordinary drying with heat changes most foods so that they never feel or taste the same again. Freeze-drying gives a very dry stuff which becomes just like the original food when the water is put back.

You might like to know that very tiny organisms like bacteria can be preserved for years by freeze-drying. Then they can be made to grow again just by adding water. However, this works only for tiny one-celled organisms. Part of the trick is freezing very quickly to keep ice crystals very small so they don't damage membranes and structures inside the cells.

How come fresh water doesn't mix with salt water?

Caleb VanderHorst
Maumee, Ohio

Actually, fresh water and salt water do mix—but not very rapidly, especially if the fresh water is on top. Because salt water has all that dissolved salt, it is more dense (heavier). That makes it go to the bottom.

But if we wait long enough, the salt and water molecules keep moving around and mixing. That's called diffusion. In time the fresh water becomes saltier, and the salt water becomes fresher, until they are just alike.

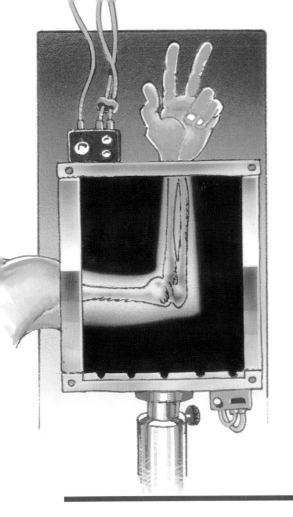

How come when you take an x-ray the skin doesn't show up?

Simone Seikaly
Salt Lake City, Utah

The answer depends on the nature of x-rays. They can be thought of as a very special kind of light, though a kind of light our eyes cannot see.

Light behaves as if it travels in little packets of energy called photons. Each photon of an x-ray has thousands of times more energy than a photon of ordinary light we can see. Because it has so much energy, it is hard to stop. Another way to say this is that x-rays are very penetrating.

Soft or less dense materials like paper or wood or rubber do not stop many x-ray photons. Most of them go on through. Hard and more dense materials like rocks or metals or bones are more likely to stop x-rays. So an x-ray photograph just shows the shadows of the more dense materials that were in the way. Skin and blood and muscle are not nearly as dense as bone. So an x-ray photograph usually shows most clearly the shadows of the bones.

If we can correct people's eyesight with glasses, can't we make glasses that have x-ray vision?

Naomi Cohl
Oakland, New Jersey

It is fun to think about being able to wear glasses that would allow you to look right through things by seeing x-rays. There is a very simple reason why this would never work in everyday life.

Our eyes see light only when there is light around us. The eyes do not put out anything. They are only receivers and detectors of light. During the day there is lots of light around us, but at night we have to use lamps to make light if we want to see.

The amount of x-radiation around us is very small—too small even to measure. Of course we can make "lamps" to produce x-rays that are used medically to photograph bones in our bodies. But a whole lot of x-radiation is bad for us. If there were enough x-radiation around us to use for seeing, I doubt that there would be any humans or other living things on earth.

So I am happy just to be able to see with light.

I like science and want to be a scientist when I grow up. But I don't know the things that will make me one. Can you help?

David Kuric
Vista, California

There isn't one special answer that will work for everyone, but I can give you some ideas. Start with a particular part of nature—the world around you—that you can learn about and understand.

Here are some suggestions. How about birds? Ask your mom or dad if you can put up a bird feeder. Then try to find someone in your neighborhood who is a bird watcher and can teach you about the birds.

How about numbers? You may think that addition and subtraction and fractions are pretty dull. But you will be surprised if you start doing puzzles and games with them. Numbers can be fun.

How about stars? Look for someone in your neighborhood who can help you pick out stars and constellations.

There are lots of ideas like these that will be fun and teach you things you will never learn from books. Books are not science. They only help you understand it.

41

I read an article about the South Pole. It looks freezing cold! If it is warm down south, why does it look so cold at the South Pole?

Karl Saxon
Mobile, Alabama

We are so used to living in the Northern Hemisphere that we forget to think about how things work in the Southern Hemisphere. You are correct that as you go south from where we live, the weather is likely to get warmer. That happens until you get to the equator. Then as you keep going south the weather is likely to get colder again as you get closer to the South Pole.

The coldest places on the earth are likely to be near the North and South Poles. Actually, I think the coldest place on earth is often somewhere on the continent of Antarctica, not very far from the South Pole.

If the world is round, wouldn't the people in the southern part be upside-down?

Katie Jagielski
West Allis, Wisconsin

The hardest part of getting used to the idea that the earth is round is that upside-down part. First you have to ask the meaning of "up" and "down."

The earth is a very large ball. Everything on it is pulled toward its center by the force of gravity. "Down" is "toward the ground," which is also toward the center of the earth. "Up" is away from the ground.

This works wherever you are, at every place on the earth's surface. There is no place you can stand on your feet on the earth's surface and be upside-down.

How do you get to China by digging a hole?

Lee Delattre
Ayer, Massachusetts

When you get to thinking about the earth as a big ball, you naturally begin to wonder about digging a hole through it from one side to the other. The idea of doing that is perfectly

OK. The practical problem of doing it is so great that no one has ever tried in any really serious way.

One very practical problem is that the center of the earth seems to be a very hot molten mass that would melt any tools you can imagine using. And I guess it would cook anyone who was trying to use them.

So the idea of digging a hole through the earth probably will always be just an idea.

43

Why is it that if you drop an object into water, it falls quickly until it hits the water?

Jill Kress
Pittsburgh, Pennsylvania

You are quite right about your observation. You can feel it happen every time you dive into a swimming pool. You suddenly slow down when you hit the water.

You are talking about an interesting property of fluids. Both air and water are fluids because both of them can flow. Some fluids flow more easily than others. Air flows more easily than water. (And water flows more easily than pancake syrup.)

When you are diving through air, the air is pushed to the side and must flow around you. It's so easy that it only feels like wind going by. Once you hit the water, however, the water must flow around you. And water does not flow so easily. That's what slows you down.

I have never dived into pancake syrup, but I think I wouldn't want to. That would really slow you down.

Whenever I get my hair wet, it is darker than when it is dry. Why?

Jane Boyer
Festus, Missouri

Many things are darker when wet. Garden soil is, and paper is, too. I was surprised how much darker white Kleenex is when you make a wet spot on it.

If something gets darker, that means it is reflecting less light to your eye. Evidently a wet surface tends to trap light better and doesn't bounce it off as well. I think that may be why your hair looks darker when wet.

Why is it that when water comes down a waterfall it turns white?

Nancy Meadows
Crownsville, Maryland

I had never thought about that before so I wondered about it for a while. I am not sure of the answer, but I think it is something like this.

Light is reflected from a quiet pool of water as if the surface were a mirror. But if water is broken up enough into droplets, then there are many small pieces of water surface reflecting light at many different angles. Such a surface looks white.

You might think of glass that is clear and colorless. Some of the light that falls upon it is reflected from its smooth surface. But if the glass is ground or "frosted" to give it a rough surface, then it also looks white.

So I think that clouds and waterfalls look white because their water droplets make many little mirrors reflecting light in all directions. The many little water surfaces make what is called a diffuse reflector.

I've always wondered how the shape of a rainbow is formed.

Tom Harkman
Monticello, Minnesota

You also could ask why rainbows are always in the form of a bow or arc. Actually, they are always pieces of a circle.

A rainbow is made by rays of light from the sun which are bent and reflected by raindrops so that they come back to your eyes. Blue-violet light is bent more than red, so you see a band of light with all the colors in between spread out in order.

When you see a rainbow, the sun is always behind you and low in the sky. Imagine that you are holding your left hand in front of you so that it is in the shadow of your head. Now imagine that you use your right hand to point at the outer edge of the rainbow. And now keep your right hand pointing at the red part but move it back and forth from one end of the rainbow to the other. You will see that your right hand is moving in a circle. The angle between your hands will always be 42 degrees.

Why 42 degrees? That is the special angle at which red light comes back to you from raindrops. The only raindrops that can do that for you are at special places in the sky that make a circle. That's the circle which your right hand pointed to. Blue-violet light is bent at a smaller angle of about 40 degrees so it appears as a smaller, inside circle. Try that on your next rainbow.

If ultraviolet and infrared rays are invisible, how do we know about them?

Diana Foss
Huntington Beach, California

The best answer is that we know about them because of what they do. We have ways to detect and measure them.

Light that we can see is a very small part of what is called electromagnetic radiation. Radiation can be thought of as wave motion. We talk about different kinds of radiation which are really different only in how closely packed together their waves are. So we talk about their wavelength.

X-rays are very closely packed waves with short wavelength. And radio waves have a very long wavelength. In between there is the special region of wavelength where the radiation behaves like light. An even smaller region is one our eyes can see. That is what we call visible light.

Light that your eye can see comes in different colors, from the shorter wavelength violet, through blue, green, and yellow, to the longer wavelength red. So we say that light of wavelengths too short to see is ultraviolet (shorter than violet). And light of wavelengths too long to see is infrared (longer than red).

A radio can detect radio waves, and we have many gadgets that can detect and measure light. Seeing light with the eye is only one way we have of measuring it.

Why are the sky and water blue?

Lisa Marse
Metairie, Louisiana

The answers are not quite the same. The sky is blue because of the small scattering of sunlight by molecules of gases in the air, mostly by nitrogen molecules. We think of air as being very clear and transparent—and it is. We think of sunlight as being almost white—and it is. But in going thousands of miles through our atmosphere a tiny amount of sunlight is scattered. When that happens blue light rays are scattered more than red light rays—in fact about six times more.

So the light that is scattered down to us from the sky looks blue. I'm glad that happens. If it did not, the sky would look black.

Water is blue for a different reason. Of course when you look at the ocean or a big lake it may look blue partly because of light reflected back from the sky. But water is blue mostly because it *is* blue. You can't see this just looking through a glass of water. But try looking through the water in a clear lake or in a swimming pool that has white sides and bottom. If you look through enough clear water you will see that it is blue.

Water, even very pure water, absorbs red light rays a little more than blue rays. So water is a little bit blue.

When I sit by my window, I wonder how many different gases there are. Do you know all of the gases? I want to know.

Becky Lessing
San Antonio, Texas

If you look out the window at all the air around you, there is nothing to see. So what are all the gases out there?

There are a lot of gases in the air around us. Of course, most of the air is made up of just three gases—nitrogen, oxygen, and argon. There are smaller amounts of carbon dioxide and water vapor. And there are about ten more gases in amounts so tiny that people seldom talk about them. Of course, the list doesn't stop, either. Anything that you can smell—like roses or cheese or onions—must have some chemical that is carried as a gas in the air. So if you want to think of things like that, then the list of gases in the air would go on and on. I hope you do not want me to name them all because I doubt that anyone really knows.

Why doesn't the earth's oxygen get used up, since everybody breathes it?

Vivek Dehejia
Nepean, Ontario

You are right that we use up a lot of oxygen. Each person needs about five hundred quarts or over a pound of oxygen every day. If you think of all the people in the world doing that—and all the other animals, too—that's a lot of oxygen.

Fortunately there is a very neat answer to this problem. All of the green plants in the world are making oxygen. Not only that, but we animals are making the carbon dioxide that plants need. So plants and animals live happily together by swapping those two gases back and forth.

The concentration of oxygen in air is about 20.94 percent. That value has not changed in all the years it has been measured, so our recycling of oxygen must be working very well.

I was looking at our wood stove and I noticed that the flame was kind of blue. How come?

Rebekah Rooh
Forest Grove, Oregon

Most gases burn with a blue flame. Wood burns best when it gets hot enough to turn the wood into a gas, which then burns in the flame. Your wood stove must do a good job of burning wood.

I think you asked your question because we are used to seeing the yellow flames of an open bonfire. I think the yellow comes from glowing particles of carbon that are carried into the flame.

Why do things rust?

Melissa Riley
Oakville, Missouri

You may have noticed that rusty things are made of iron. When iron is in contact with air, it actually burns very slowly to make iron oxide. That's the red stuff you call rust. Things rust much more rapidly in the presence of water.

The reaction with oxygen can occur only at the surface of the iron. Then the rust usually crumbles away, and that makes more new surface. Given enough time, an iron object like a nail may turn completely to rust.

Other metals like aluminum also react with oxygen at the metal surface. But aluminum oxide sticks onto the metal and forms a protective coat.

49

Please explain why balloons float to the ground softly, like parachutes.

Ian Nichols
Canoga Park, California

When you blow up a balloon by mouth, it is full of air. The rubber doesn't weigh very much. The whole balloon is only a little heavier than the same volume of air. So it does sink to the ground. But as it sinks it must push a lot of air out of the way.

You might try this experiment. You need two rubber balloons that are just alike. Blow up one of them. Leave the other without being blown up. Now drop both balloons and watch how they fall. A balloon that's not blown up falls like most other objects, but the blown-up balloon just floats to the ground.

You are right about parachutes. Even when attached to a weight, they float down like a balloon because they must push away so much air.

Why do airplanes sometimes leave white streaks in the air?

Michelle Patano
Schaumburg, Illinois

The engines of a jet plane are burning a lot of fuel. The burning process makes carbon dioxide and water. Most jets fly pretty high, like 35,000 feet, where the air is cold. The water vapor coming out of the jet engines rapidly condenses to form water droplets. So the plane forms a long narrow cloud behind it, which makes a white streak across the sky.

Sometimes, when there is enough water vapor in the high-up sky, another effect also takes place. The high-speed movement of the plane cools the air behind it enough to make the water vapor condense into tiny water droplets.

Why is a cast-iron pan heavy when I carry it by the handle and light when I carry it by the handle and the front part?

Sara Busby
Willow, Alaska

I think you have made an important observation. There are easier ways and harder ways to carry something. It is hard to hold a heavy pan by its handle if it is straight out in front of you. The muscles of your hand and arm must hold up the weight of the pan. They also must work extra hard to hold it in that awkward position. If you just hold the pan by its handle and let the pan swing downward, it will be easier to hold in that position.

The actual weight of the pan doesn't change. But your muscles have to work harder to hold it in some positions. If you watch workers who carry ladders or heavy bags of cement or heavy tools, you will see that they have special ways of carrying those things. They have learned to use the easiest way.

When we look at the sun, it's a big ball. Why do they say it's no bigger or different from any other star?

Margaret Malave
Carteret, New Jersey

Even though the sun is 93 million miles away, it still looks like a big ball. But it is not really unusually bright compared to other stars. It is just closer to us.

Other stars that you can see are likely to be brighter than the sun, but more than 100,000 times as far away. It is the distance that fools you. The universe is a big place.

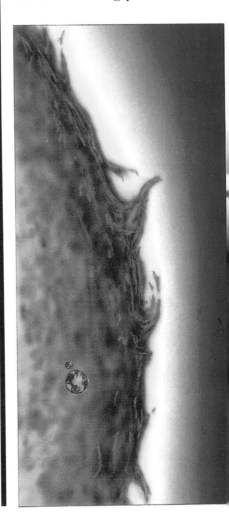

I would like to know if space ever stops.

Dorian Watson
Plano, Texas

That is about the biggest question in science, because the universe is the biggest thing we know of. I doubt that anyone really knows the answer.

I have read some ideas about this. One is that the universe is constantly expanding. Another is that space is really curved. I think this means that lines which seem straight to us must actually bend in the great distance of space and curve back to make great curves or circles. Another idea is that there is a real edge to the universe, but so far away no one could ever find it.

However, all of these are just ideas and I think the best answer to your question is that no one knows.

When I clap my hands, they make a different sound each time. How do they do that?

Larissa Young
Aliquippa, Pennsylvania

I had never thought about that question, so I tried clapping in different ways. You are right. My hands make different sounds depending on how I clap them. Most of the noise made by clapping comes from the air that is squeezed and compressed as your hands come together. You might think of the noise made by bursting a balloon or by breaking a blown-up paper bag. Balloons and paper bags are not themselves very noisy. Breaking them sends out a sudden pressure wave into the air. And that's what sound really is.

The palms of your hands are somewhat cup-shaped, so they are good at compressing air when they come together. That's the loudest clap you can make. The quietest clap you can make is to spread out the fingers of both hands and just let your fingers come together. You can see why they can't compress much air and make much noise.

When you're in an airplane, why do your ears pop?

Jocelyn Coe
Houston, Texas

I think I know what you mean, although my ears just hurt instead of popping. I always carry chewing gum in a plane because chewing helps.

Inside your eardrums are air-filled chambers. The chambers are connected by little open tubes to the air space in the back of your nose. In a plane that flies high-up, the cabin is pressurized so that its air pressure is higher than the outside air but usually less than at ground level. When the plane goes up, the cabin air pressure decreases and some air slowly escapes from your inner ear through the little tubes.

For many people the problem occurs when the plane comes down and air pressure in the cabin increases. The little tubes from the nose may not let air through fast enough. Then the air pressure in your inner ear stays low and the higher pressure of the cabin air pushes in on your eardrum. That hurts.

It helps to keep the muscles of your face and mouth working to massage the little tubes and keep them open for air to go through. That's why it helps to chew gum.

Does food taste the same to animals as it does to me?

Yisrael Jaeger
Far Rockaway, New York

I like your question because it comes just from curiosity of wondering. But it's also a question I can't answer. And I doubt that anyone in the world can answer it. We just have no way to tell.

There's another question like that about animals seeing. We can do experiments to find that an animal like a dog does see colors. But even after we know that, we can't tell how the world really looks to a dog.

Where does the weight go when you lose it?

Magdalena Zbierski
New York, New York

Your body is a machine, of course a very special machine. But like other machines, it needs energy to keep it working. It gets the energy by burning the foodstuffs that you eat to make carbon dioxide and water. Your largest amount of weight loss is in the carbon dioxide you breathe out.

Your weight really doesn't change much from day to day. So the gains and losses are pretty closely balanced. Your income of food and water is balanced by your losses in urine, feces, and the carbon dioxide and water breathed out of your lungs.

One way to tell about the loss of carbon dioxide and water that you breathe out is to weigh yourself carefully when you go to bed and again when you wake up. If you have a good bathroom scale, you may be able to tell that you lose almost a pound during the night.

55

Is there any object in the world with only one side?

*Gevonne Forguson
Sanford, Florida*

I don't really know how to answer that because I am not sure just what you mean by a side. How many sides does a ball have? If we should decide that it has only one, then we would say that the whole earth has only one side. That is, unless you think about the idea of inside and outside.

I also thought about the Mobius strip that you may know about. It is easy to make.

Take a strip of paper, twist it once, and then tape its ends together. If you trace your finger along one side, you will touch every surface before coming back to the place you started from. So it has only one side. Of course, this is not quite fair because it also has one edge, which might be called a side.

I'm not sure whether I answered your question, but maybe you can have some fun thinking about it.

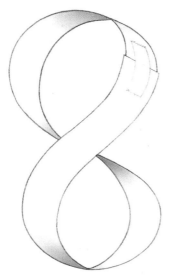

How is a car run by a motor?

*Sarah Morgan
Myakka City, Florida*

That's a big question. I can't tell you all about it, but I hope I can give you an idea.

You know that your car needs gasoline to run. The gasoline is turned into a gas or vapor, mixed with air, and carried into little chambers inside the motor. Then a spark is used to light the gas and explode it right inside each little chamber. Each explosion pushes on a crank and makes it go round and round. The sparks to the different chambers are timed just right so that they explode and push at just the right times. Then they suck in some more of the air and gas and get ready to do it all over again. That way they all work in perfect teamwork to make your car go.

Does sound travel in space?

Rachelle Theisen
Fargo, North Dakota

Sound is carried as a wave of compression in some material. The sounds we usually hear are carried by air. Space is close to a perfect vacuum, meaning there's almost nothing there. So sound does not travel in space. There is no sense in yelling at a star.

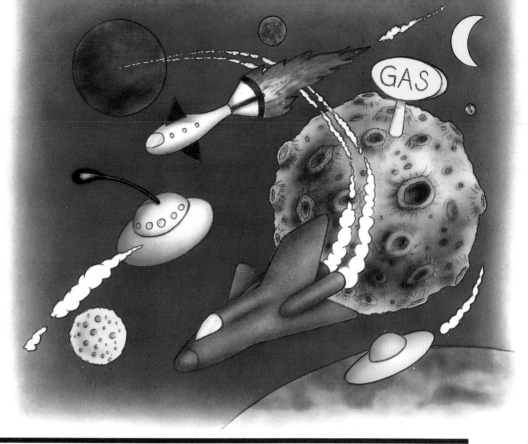

Why do we hear the sound of the ocean in seashells when they are dry?

Steve Swerdlow
Los Angeles, California

Seashells do not really make any sounds of their own. Inside they have many hard, curved surfaces which are good reflectors for sound. So any sound waves that get inside are jumbled up by all kinds of echoes. When you hold the shell up to your ear, you hear the noise of all those jumbled-up echoes. That does sound much like the noise of ocean waves beating against a shore.

If you have a seashell with a big cavity inside, try it out again at home next to your ear. Unless you get in a very, very quiet place, it will keep roaring as if it had brought some of the ocean with it.

How does smoke disappear?

Todd Fur-Marski
Manhattan Beach, California

Smoke is made up of tiny particles, usually of two kinds. One kind is made of ash, stuff not burned in the fire. The other kind of particles are tiny droplets of water which are formed when most things burn. Both kinds of particles must be small enough and light enough to get carried upward in the draft of hot air rising from the fire.

Each of the particles is too small for the eye to see. You see them as smoke only when there are lots of them together.

As the smoke rises above a chimney, it begins to mix with the air around it. The water droplets really do disappear because they evaporate to become water vapor.

The ash particles actually do not disappear. They just get farther and farther apart as they mix into the air. When they spread apart far enough they become part of the dust that is in the air all around us. They seem to have disappeared.

How does a camera put pictures on a piece of paper?

Robert Lopez
Leesburg, Indiana

You have noticed the lens on the front of a camera. It works to make an image on the back of the camera, a picture of what the camera is looking at. At the back of the camera is a film, a clear plastic sheet treated with special light-sensitive chemicals. "Light-sensitive" means that the chemicals undergo chemical reactions only when light hits them. Light-sensitive chemicals will make lighter and darker places on the film to form a picture.

These are only the basic ideas of how a camera works. You will find more about it in an encyclopedia, usually under "photography."

Why is it when you hold writing up to a mirror it is written backwards?

Nicole and Brad Van Pelt
Lisle, Illinois

The reason is that a flat mirror bounces light rays from an object back to you in straight lines. When you look in a mirror, the "you" you see is backwards, really reversed right and left.

Here's a way to check this out. Stand in front of a mirror and hold a penny out where you can see it in your right hand. Now look at yourself in the mirror. If you think about the person looking back at you, you will see that the hand holding the penny seems to be the left hand. In order to see why this happens, you must trace the course of a light ray from the penny to your eyes. The ray must go from the real penny to the point on the mirror where you see the penny and then back to your eye.

What we are talking about is called a mirror image. Because that image is reversed from the real you, a mirror cannot show you exactly how you look to other people.

59

Why do some cereals pop when you put milk on them?

Eddie Fuhrman
Gillett, Arkansas

Since I was not sure of an answer, I wrote to a company which makes breakfast cereals. Here is what they said:

Most cereal grains contain starch. It is possible to process the grains to make air pockets surrounded by starch. When starch gets wet it swells up. Then the air pockets break to give the popping noise.

I realize that this does not really tell us all that we would like to know. But at least we can understand the idea.

Our class has been studying science. I don't understand what inertia is and what momentum is.

Lisa Matthew
Alamogordo, New Mexico

The idea about inertia applies to movable things like balls and bats and cars and planes. Anything that is at rest stays at rest unless something else gives it a push. Then it is a moving body. And when in motion, it tends to keep moving in a straight line unless some force pushes or pulls to stop it or make it turn.

So the idea about inertia is simply that something tends to keep on doing whatever it is doing.

When something is moving it has momentum. The heavier it is and the faster it is moving, the harder it is to stop. So momentum is a kind of measure of how hard it is to stop something in motion.

In everyday life there is always some resistance to movement, which we call friction. Friction is like a drag or a pull against the direction of motion. This always works to slow down something in motion and make it come to rest again.

It always sounds complicated when we try to talk about things in very general terms. The best way to understand these ideas is to watch how movable things behave.

Sometimes when I am in the car it looks like there is water up ahead on the road. When I get closer, there isn't any water at all. Why?

Jill Biegler
Boca Raton, Florida

I have noticed that, too. I think you will find that it usually happens on a warm day when the sun is making the road surface hot. Then air is rising from the hot surface and other air is moving in to take its place. So there are a lot of hot and cool air drafts churning around close to the road surface. Light going through that churning air is bent back and forth to make the road surface look wavy—like a water surface.

On a hot day in the desert you might see even stranger things. They are called mirages—all kinds of strange things that seem to appear and disappear. Mixtures of churning air can bend light rays to give all sorts of strange effects.

61

My class did a science experiment with ice cubes. My group was freezing hot water and cold water to see which would freeze first. The hot-water cup froze first. The theory my group had for this was that the hot water underwent an extreme temperature change, therefore, the hot water froze first. Are we right?

Lee Ann Davis
Boulder, Colorado

In general, hot water will not freeze faster than cold water. In order to freeze hot water you have to take more heat away and usually that takes longer. So if hot water freezes faster, that is a surprise.

There are some special conditions under which hot water might freeze faster. Suppose you put exactly a pint of water in each of two identical pans and put the pans outside on a very cold day in the winter. Everything is alike except that one pan has hot water and the other pan has cold water. It is said that the pan of hot water will freeze first.

There are two possible reasons for this surprising result. First, water expands when heated. A pint of hot water really does not contain as many water molecules as a pint of cold water. So the pan of hot water will not make as much ice. Secondly, hot water will evaporate more as it is cooling down. Again this means that there will be less ice to freeze. So it is said that the pan of hot water will freeze first.

This experiment we talked about is supposed to have been reported first by a scientist, Roger Bacon, who lived in England about seven hundred years ago. I remember once reading a little article in a scientific magazine which said the experiment does not always work the way Roger said it did. The article was titled "Roger Bacon Was Mistaken."

Why is it that when you leave a glass of cold pop out it gets warm, but if you leave a hot cup of cocoa out it gets cold?

Erin DeWald
South Bend, Indiana

The way you said that does make it seem like magic. Actually that's exactly what must happen. It all depends on the way heat behaves: it always flows from someplace hotter toward someplace colder.

For something hot like cocoa, the heat flows from the cocoa to the air of the room. So the cocoa cools down. If you leave it overnight it will become the same temperature as the surrounding air.

Room air is warmer than cold pop. So heat flows from room air to the pop, and the pop warms up. If you leave the pop overnight, it will have time to reach the same temperature as the surrounding air (and the cocoa).

You can see that heat behaves logically but not magically.

Why is it that when I take a shower, the cold water faucet has drops of water on it and the hot water faucet is all steamy?

Meg Hazel
West Columbia, South Carolina

When you are in a partly closed space (like a shower) with warm water, the air gets very humid. That means that the warm air has a lot of water vapor. If there is some cold spot, water condenses out of the air to form drops of water. You can see that this is likely to happen on the cold water faucet but not on the hot water faucet.

Index

Airplanes
Pages 50, 54

Animals
Pages 21, 55

Balance
Page 37

Balloons
Pages 37, 50

Bouncing
Page 26

Breathing
Pages 34, 48

Bubbles
Pages 12, 13

Cameras
Page 58

Cars
Pages 8, 56, 61

Cereal
Page 60

Clapping
Page 53

Colors
Pages 10, 14, 18, 19, 23, 44, 45, 46, 47, 49

Constellations
Page 31

Dust
Page 17

Electricity
Pages 14, 15

Fans
Page 29

Fire
Pages 6, 27, 49, 58

Freeze-drying
Page 39

Fruit
Page 10

Gases
Pages 6, 13, 25, 48, 49

Gravity
Pages 36, 37, 43, 50

Heat
Pages 7, 15, 19, 28, 29, 33, 63

Ice
Pages 6, 7, 11, 24, 62

Inertia
Page 60

Light
Pages 9, 17, 18, 19, 40, 45, 46, 47

Magnets
Page 32

Mirages
Page 61

Mirrors
Page 59

Momentum
Page 60

Moon
Pages 8, 20, 21

Oxygen
Pages 10, 48

Pine trees
Page 11

Plants
Pages 10, 11

Popcorn
Page 5

Radiators
Page 28

Rainbows
Page 46

Rust
Page 49

Seashells
Page 57

Shivering
Page 34

Shocks
Page 14

Sight
Pages 8, 9, 40, 52, 59, 61

Smoke
Page 58

Soda
Pages 13, 63

South Pole
Page 42

Sound
Pages 22, 53, 57, 60

Space
Pages 30, 36, 52, 57

Stained glass
Page 23

Stars
Pages 9, 31, 52

Sun
Pages 8, 18, 36, 46, 52

Tape recorders
Page 15

Taste
Page 55

Tides
Page 20

Water
Pages 6, 25, 30, 38, 39, 44, 45, 47, 61, 62, 63
see also Ice

Weight
Pages 51, 55

Wind
Page 16

X-rays
Pages 40, 47